# BEN SHAHN · PAINTINGS

*Also by James Thrall Soby:* Ben Shahn: His Graphic Art

# BEN SHAHN

## PAINTINGS

*Text by James Thrall Soby*

GEORGE BRAZILLER INC·NEW YORK·1963

*For information address the publisher:*
*George Braziller, Inc.*
*215 Park Avenue South,*
*New York 3, New York*
*Library of Congress Catalogue Card Number: 63-18187*
*First Printing*

•

*Printed in heliogravure by Draeger Frères, Paris, France;*
*and in letterpress by The Haddon Craftsmen, Scranton, Pennsylvania.*
*Text set in Century Expanded and display in*
*Microgramma Bold Extended.*

•

*Format by Will Burtin.*

# CONTENTS

**ACKNOWLEDGMENTS**

*The names of owners of paintings
illustrated here
are recorded with the illustrations.
To them is due a debt of gratitude
not only for permission to publish
but also in many instances
for helpful information and aid in obtaining photographs.*

*Particular thanks are due
Mrs. Edith Gregor Halpert
and the staff of The Downtown Gallery
for their unfailing co-operation
in the preparation of this book.*

BEN SHAHN'S long and distinguished career has been marked by a number of turning points. Perhaps the first of importance occurred in 1929. He had just returned to America from two extended trips abroad which took him to France, Italy, Spain, and North Africa. He had been exposed to many of the most advanced developments in European painting of our century, and had been especially impressed by the separate talents of Rouault and Dufy. Yet one suspects that even during his excited travels he was troubled by the prevailing estheticism of the school of Paris. His own background tended to lead him in an opposite direction. Born in Kovno, Russia (Lithuania), in 1898, he had come to Brooklyn, New York, in 1906 and grown up with his Jewish family in rather impoverished circumstances. As a very young child in Russia he had drawn incessantly, and in Brooklyn he was often forced by local toughs to make sidewalk chalk sketches of various heroes of the sports world of the day. It is safe to assume that the drawings were not made entirely under duress. Shahn has always had a profound interest in flamboyant, contemporary personalities and in recording them with imaginative rather than literal precision.

9

As to precision, we must remember that Shahn's training as a graphic artist has been exceptionally thorough. From 1913 to 1917 he worked as a lithographer's apprentice during the day, while attending high school at night, and he supported himself through lithography until roughly 1930. Whereas most artists with his inventive gifts would have found the exact requirements of commercial lithography deadening, Shahn seems to have respected his task. There remained the problem of how to put his instinctive love of accuracy to creative rather than documentary use. It was this problem that he began to solve in 1929, after several years of study at New York University, the City College of New York, and the National Academy of Design, and after his two trips to Europe and North Africa (1925 and 1927). In 1930 he went to Truro on Cape Cod. There he made up his mind. "I had seen all the right pictures and read all the right books—Vollard, Meier-Graefe, T. E. Hulme," he recalls, "but still it didn't add up to anything. 'Here am I,' I said to myself, 'thirty-two years old, the son of a carpenter. I like stories and people. The French school is not for me.'"

THE QUESTION remained as to how realism could regain for him the validity that it lacked for most of his contemporaries. In his quest for a solution he was undoubtedly encouraged by the photographer, Walker Evans, with whom at that time he shared a studio on Bethune Street in Greenwich Village, and a cottage at Truro on Cape Cod. Evans, for his part, was determined to turn his back on the artful manipulations of many contemporary photographers and to record with the maximum directness those commonplace but evocative aspects of the living scene which the maestros of photography considered beneath the dignity of their medium. Both Shahn and Evans have always shown an exceptional sensitivity to the revelatory moment and happening; both, in their separate media, have made this sensitivity the sinew of their expression.

If 1929 marked the beginning of Shahn's awareness of what art could and should be for him, he took his first decided step forward in 1931, when he completed twelve border illustrations for an edition of the haggadah (plate 1). Previously he had made ten lithographs to illustrate De Quincey's essay, "Levana," from *Suspiria De Profundis*, but these had been rather mannered and had shown a residual influence from such members of the School of Paris as Rouault. In the haggadah illustrations, on the contrary, Shahn's own personality commences to break through the overlay of acquired stylization and to reveal an idiosyncratic impulse. And in 1931-32 he found what he needed most—a narrative subject in which he could believe profoundly. He says: "Then I got to thinking about the Sacco-Vanzetti case. . . . Ever since I could remember I'd wished that I'd been lucky enough to be alive at a great time—when something big was going on, like the Crucifixion. And suddenly I realized I was. Here I was living through another crucifixion. Here was something to paint!" Over a period of seven months he worked on a series of twenty-three small gouache paintings and two large panels, dealing with the trial and eventual execution for murder of the American-Italian anarchists, Nicola Sacco and Bartolomeo Vanzetti.

THE PATENT INJUSTICE of the trial had aroused indignation in liberal circles throughout the world, and pictures such as the gouache: "Demonstration in Paris" (plate 2) are based on incidents Shahn had actually witnessed. He had also looked carefully at press photographs of the condemned men with their guards, and from these evolved the haunting image (plate 3) which far transcends everything in journalistic photography except its noncommittal accuracy. The characterization of the prisoners is pungent and memorable; the tragic intensity of their faces contrasts subtly with the complacent righteousness of their guards. Shahn has always been a master of telling detail, and has often used it for satirical purposes in which mannered exaggerations have no part. And we should remember, as an indication of his solitary and unrelenting faith in what he wants to say as a painter, that the Sacco-Vanzetti series was completed at precisely the moment when abstract art was enjoying one of its perennial returns to favor with the profession and the "advanced" public.

The Sacco-Vanzetti series was succeeded in 1932-33 by a group of fifteen gouache paintings and a tempera panel on the case of the persecuted labor leader, Tom Mooney, which are more fluent and richer in color than the preceding series. Before being exhibited at The Downtown Gallery in New York, they were much admired by the Mexican muralist and easel painter, Diego Rivera, who wrote the foreword to the catalogue of Shahn's show and persuaded him to become his assistant in painting a large mural fresco for Rockefeller Center in New York. (This mural was destroyed shortly after its completion because of its political content.) The image of Mooney, his mother, and wife (plate 4) is notable for its terse understatement of the anguish and bitterness felt by the labor leader and his family. In "Mooney and His Warden, J. B. Holohan" (plate 5), there exists the same attention to architectural detail which was later to be an especially compelling element in a great number of Shahn's finest pictures.

THE DEPRESSION was becoming steadily more serious, and in 1933-34 Shahn was enrolled with the Public Works of Art Project, for which he completed eight tempera paintings on the Prohibition Era. Of these, the one showing a conclave of Women's Christian Temperance Union members (plate 7) gives full play to that mordant wit which is often an earmark of Shahn's art. But in 1934-35 his mood turned sombre when the fine sketches he made with Lou Block for murals intended for Riker's Island Penitentiary were rejected by the reactionary Municipal Art Commission of New York City, though they had been approved by the Mayor and the Commissioner of Correction. These were bitter years for Shahn and, of course, for hundreds of thousands of his countrymen, and the tragic condition of the American workman is nowhere more forcefully recorded than in "Scott's Run, West Virginia" (plate 8). Yet if Shahn's sympathy for organized labor was deep and embattled, he never forgot man's individual loneliness, as in the poignant image called "Sunday Painting" (plate 9). Nor did he ever forget the solace of recreation, "Sunday Football" (plate 10) being a case in point: Its two stumpy figures peer intently through a fence and in the center of the composition occurs one of those realistic accents which the artist treasures—an actual election poster. By including it he earned a deputy sheriff's badge from its subject, one Sheriff Campbell, and lest one assume that such accents are chosen at random, it

12

should be mentioned that Shahn himself looked through his files of several thousand posters before selecting the one he reproduced on the fence of "Sunday Football."

FROM 1935 TO 1938 Shahn was employed by the Farm Security Administration as artist, designer, and, for a short time, photographer. His interest in photography dates back to his earliest years as a painter, and from his friendship with Evans, and for a long time many of his pictures were imaginative reconstructions of snapshots which he— or occasionally others—had taken. In 1937-38 came another turning point in his career when he was commissioned by the Farm Security Administration to paint a large, single-wall fresco in the community center of a federal housing development for garment workers in Roosevelt (formerly Jersey Homesteads), New Jersey. With that constancy which is so fundamental a trait, Shahn lives in the development to this day—his neighbors as much his treasured friends as certain of the professors in nearby Princeton University.

The composition of the mural at Roosevelt (plate 11) follows the undulant principle Shahn had learned from Diego Rivera: deep recessions of space alternating with human and architectural details projected forward. At the left, immigrants from Europe follow the immortal Einstein down a gangplank, away from Jew-baiting Germany, their new hopes qualified by the coffins of the American martyrs, Sacco and Vanzetti, which they have passed. Once inside the United States, in the next panel to the right, they find the grim realities of labor conditions that had so long existed here—lightless sweatshops, inadequate housing, tedious and backbreaking work with outmoded tools. Then the forces of reform begin to have their effect, as a crowd gathers symbolically before the scene of the Triangle Shirtwaist Company's disastrous fire (which led to the first cohesive protests and organized actions of the International Ladies Garment Workers Union), and listens to the exhortations of a labor leader who resembles John L. Lewis. Finally, at the right end of the mural, labor's long struggle is won, bringing new buildings, co-operative stores, and efficient schools. In the last panel, under a poster of Roose-

13

velt, whom Shahn revered, appears the ground plan of Jersey Homesteads itself, and seated around a drafting board are the figures of John Brophy, Sidney Hillman, David Dubinsky, Senator Robert F. Wagner, and that remarkable apostle of social progress, Heywood Broun. The sequence of details and the alternations of scale are handled with extreme skill. Indeed, the mural remains one of this country's most eloquent visual projections of that immense and heartening social upheaval which was the Depression's one commendable product.

IN 1938 SHAHN and his wife, Bernarda Bryson, were commissioned by the Section of Fine Arts, Public Buildings Administration, U.S. Treasury, to paint thirteen large fresco panels for the main lobby of the Bronx Central Annex Post Office in New York (plates 14 and 15). The panels were completed in August, 1939—a stupendous achievement when one considers their scale, their abundant detail, and their atmospheric warmth. In contrast to the single-wall fresco at Roosevelt, New Jersey, with its overt social message, the Bronx frescoes comprise a panorama of American agriculture and industry, their protagonists being factory workers and farmers. "My idea," the artist has said, "was to show the people of the Bronx something about America outside New York."

Shahn and his wife, who is also a very fine draftsman, succeeded in their exalted aim. The contrasts between deep perspective and close-up figures are managed with extreme dexterity, and there is, throughout, an uncanny sensitivity to lighting effects, whether natural in source, as in the agricultural scenes, or artificial, as when the flames of a blast furnace illuminate steel girders and the face of a worker. On a very large scale the murals typify what has been a constant of Shahn's esthetic—a love of evocative juxtaposition. "Most important," he once said, "is always to have a play back and forth, back and forth. Between the big and the little, the light and the dark, the smiling and the sad. . . . I like to have three vanishing points in one plane, or a half dozen in three planes." To which might be added that Shahn has always loved oppositions between inanimate rigidity and human warmth. In the Bronx panel called

14

"Textile Mills" (plate 14), for example, the definition of the bobbins, the architecture, and the metal sign is extremely precise, whereas the figure of the worker is softly rounded in contour. The Bronx murals as a whole abound in such subtle shifts of technique and mood, yet they arrive at a cohesive monumentality far more pronounced and impressive than that of his earlier mural in Roosevelt.

DESPITE HIS STRENUOUS LABORS on the Bronx frescoes, Shahn concurrently produced a surprising number of other works. In 1939, again for the Treasury's Section of Fine Arts, whose director, Edward P. Rowan, was one of the artist's most stalwart patrons and an unusually perceptive champion of contemporary painting, he completed nine sketches for a projected series of murals on the theme of the Four Freedoms. The murals were intended for the post office at St. Louis, Missouri, but the sketches were rejected on political grounds and the project was abandoned. Perhaps Shahn found some minor consolation in the fact that this same year he was commissioned by the Section of Fine Arts to paint an over-door panel on canvas for the post office at Jamaica, Long Island.

The year 1939 was also one of Shahn's most active years as an easel painter, probably because he was getting ready for a one-man show to be held at the Julien Levy Gallery, New York, in 1940—his first exhibition of the kind in seven years. At that time he painted "Seurat's Lunch" (plate 16), in which the speckled façade that characterizes so many cheap urban restaurants in this country was used in humorous reference to the great Post-Impressionist's Pointillism. The morose figure who sits in front of the restaurant, of which he is presumably the proprietor, is hauntingly lethargic, his mood emphasized by the use of printed lettering on the window which reaffirms Shahn's persistent interest in iconographical details of this kind. In another painting of this period, Shahn captures the pathos and incongruous variety of a commercial photographer's window display (plate 17), and in a third he comments satirically but good-naturedly on the truncated variants of the living human form, which have absorbed many of the best sculptors of this and earlier epochs (plate 18).

15

As a possibly helpful biographical note, it must be added that Shahn's 1940 exhibition won the serious attention of a wide professional audience of museum curators, an attention that now extends from coast to coast, so that the artist is represented today in most of the major art institutions in the country. From the 1940 show two now famous works were acquired at once by important museums: "Vacant Lot" (plate 19), with its solitary boy playing ball against a wall; and "Handball" (plate 20), whose lively counterpoint of athletic pose and evocative asymmetry of architectural detail have made it, to the painter's understandable distress, a trademark of his pictorial style. The picture is admittedly a remarkable image, proposing a curious and intensely personal amalgam of realism and fantasy, but it by no means illustrates the breadth of Shahn's achievement—especially during the past twenty-five years, when he has grown enormously in plasticity, humanistic depth, and richness of tone.

FROM 1940 TO 1942 Shahn worked with rare concentration on fresco murals for the main corridor of the Federal Security Building in Washington, D.C. (at that time known as the Social Security Building). Once more the commission had come from the Treasury's Section of Fine Arts. This time the artist made convincing use of some subjects he had already treated in easel paintings. Thus on one wall (plate 22) we find one of the figures from an easel work of 1940 called "Willis Avenue Bridge" (plate 23). In another mural (plate 21) appear, behind the basketball players in the foreground, the young athletes and the garbled architecture of "Handball" (plate 20). But these iconographical elements are interwoven with entirely new motifs. The recessions of space are even more pronounced than in the Bronx post-office murals, and there is a heightened clarity of palette, as though Shahn had abandoned atmospheric manipulations of color and light for a conciseness that recalls the Renaissance masters, Uccello and Piero della Francesca, whose masterworks Shahn had probably held in mind since his early trips to Italy.

Soon after America's entry into World War II, Shahn joined the graphic-arts division of the Office of War Information, for which he produced a number of admirable

16

posters, though only two of them were actually published and used. His talents for design and typography qualified him to an unusual degree for the task of creating posters, and his work in this medium was so exceptional that during the mid-1940's he was appointed director of the graphic-arts division of the Congress of Industrial Organizations. For this union he made some of the finest and most compelling posters yet seen in our period and country. The medium itself has been treated rather casually by most American artists; for Shahn, however, it posed a challenge he was ready to meet with the same thoughtfulness and sensitivity he applied to his easel works and his murals. Indeed, Shahn's art, whatever its eventual use, is all of one piece; its integrity is unflagging. For magazines and corporations he has provided a body of graphic work which is an extension rather than a denigration of his basic character as a painter and draftsman. Like Daumier and other fine artists before him, he has never been afraid of being sullied by the demands of the market place, and he has held firmly to standards of his own choice and belief in accepting or rejecting commissions.

IN 1944 SHAHN had another exhibition at The Downtown Gallery in New York, for which he painted a number of his most poetic images. They include the "Girl Jumping Rope" (plate 28), with its fine counterbalance of pose between the two figures and its delicacy of line in the wallpaper patterns appearing through the broken walls of the building. There was also the "Fourth of July Orator" (plate 30), in which Shahn satirically presents the orator's unthinking self-enchantment, the middle figure's dejected acceptance of duty on a public occasion, and the trained attentiveness of the figure at the left. The orator speaks to a vast, empty field, and in the distance appear the modern houses of the federal housing development at Roosevelt. Another outstanding painting of this period is the "Cherubs and Children" (plate 34), in which the color is more luminous than in perhaps any picture he had done theretofore. The same advance in tonal opulence is again obvious in the "Red Stairway" (plate 35), and it is worth noting that it was at precisely this moment that Shahn first learned how to apply translucent tones over opaque passages in tempera, thus giving his colors a new vivacity. The artist's compassionate sense of humor is given full scope in "Four Piece Orchestra" (plate 24), wherein two workmen play three instruments as an accompaniment to a cellist whose more formal clothes and sober mien suggest that he may have had some professional training, though according to Shahn himself, he was a coal miner.

During the mid-1940's, as World War II heightened from month to month in its final convulsive rage, Shahn painted a number of remarkable pictures which reflect his sympathy for Europe's anguish. In particular he concentrated on Italy; it was a country he knew and loved, and he feared for the survival of her majestic past. At this time he finished "Italian Landscape, I" (plate 32), "Italian Landscape, II" (plate 33), in which a woman carries her child across the tragic rubble toward an abandoned hotel, and "Reconstruction" (plate 37), in which Italian children play with inextinguishable absorption amid fallen masonry, while an American soldier beguiles their companions with chewing gum. The contrast between irreparable damage to ancient monuments and the gaudy self-containment of the New World's packaged goods is quite possibly intended to have ironic overtones. If so, they are tender rather than bitter, and they confirm Shahn's faith in the inherent generosity of our people.

SHAHN HAS ALWAYS had a special reverence for stone, whether in its natural or structural state, and when he painted "Liberation" (plate 38), he lavished more care on the rocks strewn in the foreground than on any other section of this masterful composition. This is a surprising fact to learn, since the figures are defined with such authority and grace. But Shahn has given the writer a firsthand account of the evolution of the picture. It was inspired by the sight of his own and his neighbors' children swinging around a pole in half-comprehending but real glee after the news had come over the radio that France was at last free of the German occupation forces. When Shahn began to paint the rubble behind the children, he used as a guide a handful a gravel brought in from his driveway. "You cannot invent the shape of a stone," he explains. And in the

18

late spring of 1945, when his attention turned to the war in the Pacific, he worked for several months on "Pacific Landscape" (plate 72), in which thousands and thousands of pebbles take on an astonishing intensity, so that they dwarf the fallen soldier and evoke an unforgettable sense of desolation and quick, unreasoning fate.

THE WAR ENDED at last. Shahn's mood lightened, and he painted the sardonic "Nearly Everybody Reads the *Bulletin*" (plate 40), the right-hand figure absurdly complacent in her newspaper hat. From 1946, too, date the colorful "World's Greatest Comics" (plate 13) and the lyric "Spring" (plate 29), in which Shahn's understanding of valid, plastic distortion is especially evident, as when he achieves a swift and convincing change of scale between the hands of the figures and the girl's lower torso and outstretched foot. His wide emotional range is summarized by two pictures of the following year: the wonderfully ludicrous "Trouble" (plate 43) and the solemn and touching image called "The Violin Player" (plate 42). Too much cannot be said about Shahn's flexibility of thought and response. If he dislikes equally the blisters of prejudice and the unguents of conformity, his love for many aspects of American life is profound and constant. It is nowhere more apparent than in "East 12th Street" (plate 44). The rather drab and even oppressive architecture of this New York block becomes elegiac because of Shahn's skill. Draftsmanship has always been the core of his style, and the authority of the far perspective in "East 12th Street" calls to mind the early work of another important artist of our time, Giorgio di Chirico.

BY THE MID-1940's, Shahn's fame, considerable for a decade, had increased enormously, and he was constantly being asked to produce works for magazines, advertising agencies, and corporations, as well as for private consumption. He met the challenge of his new eminence with firmness. As a case in point, in 1946 he was asked by the Chrysler Corporation to paint a picture which would reflect, however obliquely, the special character of an age in which the automobile plays a vital part. Many artists would not have considered such terms oppressive. But Shahn's reply to the

19

Chrysler Corporation makes plain how rigidly he has insisted on remaining his own master, whether working for himself or on commission. He wrote: "The value of any painting must . . . necessarily derive from the importance which the artist himself places on it. If he feels a powerful urgency in a situation, and if he has at his disposal the technical proficiency to realize that urgency fully, the resultant work of art will be one of value to himself and others. . . . For an artist to make a painting which is without significance to himself is simply to commercialize his past achievement." Shahn has always refused to make the slightest concession to his patrons, public and private. Thus, when the Capehart Corporation had asked him to do an advertisement for a recording of Prokofiev's *Peter and the Wolf*, he had been enthusiastic enough to create one of his most charming small paintings (plate 31), only to find that Capehart objected to some minor inaccuracy in the definition of one of the figures' sneakers. He promptly withdrew the picture and later sold it to a private collector.

This sternness of conscience has not, however, prevented Shahn from taking imaginative nourishment from many "commercial" assignments. As an example, the fine image, "Silent Music" (plate 47), was originally conceived as a drawing for the Columbia Broadcasting System's folder, "The Empty Studio." Shahn explains convincingly how and why the image turned out to be what it is—a picture of empty seats and music stands, the musicians absent: "The emotion conveyed by great symphonic music happens to be expressed in semi-mathematical acoustic intervals and this cannot be transposed in terms of ninety portraits or caricatures of performers."

EVER SINCE the closing years of World War II, Shahn's art has for the most part become steadily more fluent, and from the late 1940's date such memorable pictures as "Interior" (plate 46), with its evocative handling of a Victorian bureau derived from a drawing he had made to illustrate the story of the Hickman fire (see below). It is notable also for its skilled use of contrast in the techniques of the two religious images on the wall: the one almost pre-Raphaelite in its precision, the other forcefully crude. From this time also dates "Nocturne" (plate 41) about which the painter himself has remarked: "Whatever I feel about men who sing and play guitars I've said in the present picture." A booklet of Christmas drawings he published in 1949 led him to paint "On the First Day of Christmas" (plate 51), in which printed words are given a major importance, reminding us that Shahn is among other things a highly original typographer. And in "The Anatomical Man" (plate 45), as he has done often throughout his career, he has combined motifs from his previous paintings. This sort of anthological system could lead to coldness and repetition in less positive hands, but Shahn uses it with the same conviction that characterizes his transfer of subjects from his easel works to the murals in the Federal Security Building in Washington, D. C.

There were some critics who complained at this time that Shahn had turned his back forever on social themes. Their idea was disproved by the paintings the artist made of incidents in the Centralia Mine disaster. Nevertheless, it must be admitted that for some time Shahn had been less and less interested in social content for its own sake. In his eloquent book, *The Shape of Content* (1957), he has given a lucid and revealing account of how, when, and why this change in his philosophy took place: "I was not the only artist who had been entranced by the social dream, and who could no longer reconcile that view with the private and inner objectives of art.... The change in art, mine included, was accomplished during World War II. For me, it had begun during the late thirties when I worked in the Resettlement Administration. I had then crossed and recrossed many sections of the country, and had come to know well so many people of all kinds of belief and temperament, which they maintained with a transcendent indifference to their lot in life. Theories had melted before such experience. My own painting then had turned from what is called 'social realism' into a sort of personal realism. I found the qualities of people a constant pleasure.... There were the poor who were rich in spirit, and the rich who were also sometimes rich in spirit...."

APART FROM SHAHN'S conversion from social to what he has called personal realism, in recent years he has made frequent use of symbolism and allegory, alternating one or both of these traditional poetic devices with a more straightforward treatment of aspects of American life which have interested him. As for symbolism (we shall come to allegory in a moment), the picture from 1950 called "Epoch" (plate 50) is a case in point: on the surface this painting would seem to be merely a wonderfully gay image of three acrobats, two of them mounted on spidery bicycles, the third balanced aloft on their heads. But then one begins to ponder the title—"Epoch"—and to wonder why the cyclists hold up "Yes" and "No" signs. One notices the deathly pallor of the face of the top figure, and one realizes finally that he is Everyman, balancing precariously between the opposites of consent and dissent which exist in this epoch, as they have in nearly all others. Here again Shahn does not labor his moral point; he makes it quietly and, in this case, with relieving humor. The picture's virtue is that it can be read both as symbolism and as wit. Moreover, in a more formal sense, the painting's elisions and distortions are thoroughly heartfelt.

This same year (1950) Shahn saw and photographed near Mulberry Street in New York one of the annual festivals in honor of the early Neapolitan saint, Gennaro (St. Januarius). Soon afterward he painted a picture of the scene "Ave" (plate 53). In it, details from his photograph are referred to only obliquely, as when the maze of light bulbs that surrounded the saint's image in his photograph is transposed into an abstract tangle of wiring in the right background. The identical eight banners bearing San Gennaro's likeness could easily have become monotonous, but are given appealing variety through adroit placing and through their unpredictability in partly blocking out the faces of the dinner-jacketed men standing behind them. Shahn has always been deeply interested in the variabilities of human stance, and the postures of the two dignitaries at the right are held in subtle equation with those of the nuns hurrying toward them. The picture is rich in color, and it catches the rather incongruous spirit of American celebrations of the kind in which an audience in formal dress pays tribute to a religious figure whose character presumably stemmed from simplicity itself. "Ave" is also one of the most penetrating of the artist's works, perhaps because it reflects an atavistic fascination with pageantry on Shahn's part. And for all its complexity of detail, the picture is beautifully ordered in the plastic sense. Shahn almost always knows what to leave out, as in the fine "Composition with Clarinets and Tin Horn" (plate 61), where he realized that the face of the man behind the instruments would have proved a distracting element and therefore showed only his arms and hands.

SHAHN'S RISING INTEREST in allegory has been mentioned in passing. This interest began in 1948 when he was asked by *Harper's* Magazine to illustrate an account by John Bartlow Martin of a Chicago tenement fire in which a Negro named Hickman had lost four children, and had afterward killed the landlord because he was sure the landlord himself had set the blaze. The Hickman trial for murder (of which he was finally acquitted) had aroused public indignation, and Shahn was moved by the story, as he had been by the trial of Sacco and Vanzetti years before. But now, instead of documenting incidents of a tragic and actual event, he began to think of the fire as a beast with flaming mane. Under the belly of the animal he placed Hickman's dead children, and we have his own word that in so doing, he recalled the legend of Romulus and Remus— a legend that had horrified him as a child, since he was positive that the she-wolf would devour rather than suckle her alien young. Besides, fires were a matter of painful, personal memory for the artist. He had experienced two in his youth: the first, in his native Russia, had been merely colorful; the second, in Brooklyn, had been almost fatal to himself and his brothers and sisters, who were rescued at the last moment by their father. Perhaps only so bitter an awareness of the treachery of fire could have led Shahn to abandon factual reporting for the greater, summary power of allegory. At any rate, he soon painted the remarkable picture that he called simply "Allegory" (plate 48). In his words, it, among other paintings, led "into a series of paintings of more or less classical allusion, some only pleasant, but some . . . like the 'City of Dreadful Night' [plate 57] . . . were major paintings to me, each having, beside its classical allusion, a great deal of additional motivation."

Shahn has described the last-named picture as follows: "There was the painting called 'City of Dreadful Night'—a forest of televison aerials—lines in paint—splashes of light, or heads of ancient demons tangled in the antennae—a somber building with moldering Greek heads. All of these images arose out of paint, yes, but they also arose out of the somewhat ominous implications of television for the mind, for the culture." If we compare this picture with the "Ave" discussed earlier (plate 53), we see at once how decided was the iconographical change in Shahn's art at this juncture, though we must add at once that the change was not intended to rule out permanently his concern for the living present. His use of allegory and classical allusion continues in "Labyrinth" (plate 52), wherein the figure of Icarus plunges headfirst toward a rectangular maze. The maze is presumably a reference to the Cretan labyrinth designed by Daedalus to hold the Minotaur but which was to become his and his son Icarus' prison. In Shahn's picture, however, Icarus is already equipped with the liberating wax wings whose dissolution by the sun led to his fatal plunge into the Aegean Sea.

WHILE PAINTING the image of the animal in "Allegory," Shahn had become interested in creating a fantastic bestiary, and several years later produced such pictures as "Harpie" (plate 63). He himself wrote in *The Shape of Content:* "Among my discarded symbols pertaining to the Hickman story there were a number of heads and bodies of beasts, besides several Harpies, Furies, and other symbolic, semi-classic shapes and figures. Of one of these, a lion-like head, but still not a lion, I made many drawings, each drawing approaching more nearly some inner figure of primitive terror which I was seeking to capture. . . . Of the other symbols I developed into paintings a good menagerie of Harpies, of birds with human heads, of curious and indecipherable beasts all of which I enjoyed immensely, and each of which held just enough human association for me to be

24

great fun, and held just enough classical allusion to add a touch of elegance which I also enjoyed."

From such mythological images—and they are indeed most elegant—Shahn turned back to relative realism in "Anger" (plate 56) and the enigmatic and strangely disturbing "Age of Anxiety" (plate 64). But allegorical subjects continued to fascinate him, and in 1952 he painted "Second Allegory" (plate 54), in which a recumbent figure is menaced by a celestial apparition that points an accusing hand. Shahn has always read widely, particularly philosophical works, and in 1954 he produced his striking watercolor of Maimonides (plate 55), the twelfth-century Jewish scholar who became the Rabbi of Cairo and who tried to combine Rabbinic Judaism with Aristotle's philosophy as interpreted by the Arabic scholars under whom he had studied. The picture's careful delicacy of detail calls to mind once more the thoroughness of Shahn's technical training as a graphic artist; once more he invests typography with a courageous and inventive proficiency.

THE RANGE of Shahn's iconographical and plastic ingenuity is nowhere more apparent than in two pictures of 1954: "Incubus" and "Blind Botanist." In "Incubus" (plate 58) a bizarre nightmare figure, holding a clarinet, bestrides the troubled head of its victim. The strange make-up on the figure's face, its enormous hands, and the intricate tracery of its embroidered jacket have a hallucinatory vividness, as though Shahn himself had seen them in a dream. The face of the man the incubus torments is reduced to those essentials of characterization which the artist has used repeatedly, the dark, round accents of eyes and nostrils playing against the severe lines of the mouth and eyebrows. One could not possibly mistake the painter of this face, and part of Shahn's distinction is that his pictures are so quickly recognizable as his. Similarly, "Blind Botanist" (plate 69) carries the unmistakable mark of his highly individual style. Quite likely the reason he has had few outstanding disciples is that this style is basically inimitable, as certain followers have learned to their distress.

In 1955, continuing his alternate regard for actuality and allegory as sources of inspiration, Shahn painted the lyric

"Second Spring" (plate 66) and "Third Allegory" (plate 62). The latter picture refers in symbolic terms to the story of the ark of the covenant, a story that had affected Shahn deeply in his youth, as he has said in the following reminiscence: "In Russia I went to a Jewish school, of course, where we *really read* the Old Testament. That story was about the ark being brought into the temple, hauled by six white oxen, and balanced on a single pole. The Lord knew that the people would worry about the ark's falling off the pole, so to test their faith He gave orders that no one was to touch it, no matter what happened. One man saw it beginning to totter, and he rushed up to help. He was struck dead. I refused to go to school for a week after we read that story. It seemed so damn unfair. And it still does."

In "Third Allegory" (plate 62) Shahn's interpretation of the biblical story is, of course, thoroughly personal and fanciful. The ox bearing the slabs of the Ten Commandments becomes a chimerical beast wearing a blanket, and behind it stands a hooded figure blowing a ram's horn. The hieroglyphics of the Commandments hold the center of the composition, between the hands of the figure and the animal's head with bared fangs and tongue thrust out. The image is memorable, and it typifies the cultural profundity which accounts in part for the richness of Shahn's art.

FROM SUCH SACROSANCT THEMES the artist was capable of turning abruptly to a group of lively paintings of jazz musicians. Music, as noted before, is one of Shahn's chief delights, and musicians and musical instruments reappear constantly in his imagery, as when he paints the brilliantly colorful "Chicago" (plate 68), the rapt and thoughtful "Folk Song" (plate 70), or the fine "Lute, I" and "Lute and Molecules" (plates 80 and 82).

FOR A GROWING NUMBER of contemporary painters Goya has lately taken on renewed meaning, and in 1956, in tribute to the Spanish master, Shahn executed one of his best recent watercolors, "Goyescas" (plate 67), in which an appalling military officer holds a cat's cradle in his upstretched hands, above the littered dead. In this connection, Shahn's own words on Goya are cogent, as they are on so many subjects:

"I am plagued by an exasperating notion: What if Goya, for instance, had been granted a Guggenheim, and then, completing that, had stepped into a respectable and cozy teaching job in some small—but advanced!—New England college, and had thus been spared the agonies of the Spanish Insurrection? The unavoidable conclusion is that we would never have had 'Los Caprichos' or 'Los Desastres de la Guerra.' The world would not have been called upon to mourn for the tortured woman of the drawing inscribed 'Because She Was a Liberal!' Nor would it have been stirred by Goya's pained cry, 'Everywhere It Is The Same!' Neither would it have been shocked by his cruel depictions of human bestiality, nor warned—so graphically, so unforgettably— that fanaticism is man's most abominable trait." The moral here is a fundamental of Shahn's philosophy: that total withdrawal from the contemporary scene usually brings about art's suicide.

DURING THE PAST five or six years Shahn's imagery has broadened still further in scope and variety. He has painted such satirical works as "Cosmos" (plate 71) and "Conversations" (plate 87) ; he has made the marvelous drawing, "Third Alphabet" (plate 78), which is quite as abstract as most pictures by the so-called Action Painters of today in New York and elsewhere. He has turned again to symbolism in "Helix and Crystal" (plate 77), a work inspired by his awareness that something like ninety-seven per cent of modern research is devoted to the physical sciences (the crystal) and the meagre remainder to biological matters. In this picture man is blind, his throat is menaced by a facet of the crystal, he has no ears, only a metalic helix around his neck. The symbolical trend continues in "Parable" (plate 84), very likely the most important of all Shahn's paintings of the past few years and an extraordinarily powerful reminder of the fate mankind faces if sanity is not somehow restored to the world.

Some idea of the iconographical proficiency of Shahn's work during the past decade may be formed by even a casual glance at three paintings from this recent period. "The Defaced Portrait" of 1955 (plate 59) is as ferocious in its antimilitary acrimony as the early drawings of George

Grosz. The "Still Life With Persian Vase" (plate 86) of a few years later is, on the contrary, tender and quiet, its color exceptionally sensuous. And the "Ram's Horn and Menorah" (plate 81) reveals in full measure the trained use Shahn has always made of lettering to augment the force of his imagery. He has grown steadily more assured as an artist, without succumbing, in the process, to the glib repetition of manner and subject which has been the downfall of some of his leading colleagues here and abroad.

IN 1960-62 SHAHN completed what is probably the most eloquent series of related paintings he has done to date. The series, whether by premeditated plan or obsessional impetus, includes eleven paintings (plates 88–98), its collective title being "The Lucky Dragon." As with his pictures about the Centralia Mine disaster and the Hickman case, it was inspired by drawings he had made for *Harper's* Magazine. This time he had been asked to illustrate three articles by the physicist, Ralph E. Lapp, which appeared in *Harper's* in 1957-58. The articles describe in restrained but frightening terms the catastrophe which had befallen the Japanese fishing trawler, *"Fukuryu Maru"* ("Lucky Dragon"), in 1954. Fishing for tuna and shark out of its home port of Yaizu, the boat had sailed toward the Marshall Islands and ended up close to Bikini Atoll where, unknown to the boat's crew, the United States was testing its new H-bombs.

On March 1, 1954, the "Lucky Dragon" was covered with radioactive ashes. Its crew members became sick on the voyage home and one of them, Aikichi Kuboyama, died the following September after a long, anguished illness. His shipmates all recovered, and the question of the *direct* cause of Kuboyama's death is both academic and ironic, for there is some possibility that it was caused by hepatitis, with which he may have been infected by the blood transfusions given him in a Japanese hospital to counteract the effects of the H-bomb fallout. From all accounts, he was probably the most intelligent man in the "Lucky Dragon's" crew (he was a radio operator rather than an ordinary seaman) but, like all his shipmates, he could not at first understand what had caused the rain of ashes on his boat, and had slept with a wrapped parcel of the lethal dust under his pillow.

28

IT IS NOT KNOWN EXACTLY how many drawings Shahn made of the "Lucky Dragon" incident. We do know that when he was working on his illustrations for the article on the Centralia Mine disaster, he had turned up in Russell Lynes's office at *Harper's* with no less than sixty-four drawings; he told Lynes casually that he had about thirty more at home. This extensive accumulation of graphic imagery, whether or not in preparation for easel paintings, is by no means unique in Shahn's art. His final process of selection remains mysterious, as with most true artists. He based one of his pictures, "Why" (plate 91), on his drawing of Kuboyama's flower-strewn grave, its headstone as impressive as a carving by Brancusi or Henry Moore, though it is in fact a locally designed, communal property, long and repeatedly in use. He painted another picture—and it is one of his most poetic—to record the end of the funeral ceremony, when a flock of pigeons was released by Japanese students (plate 93).

In an early painting in the same series, Shahn was preoccupied with living terror, expressed in symbolic as opposed to the social-realist forms of his early career (plate 94). The ominous cloud that first mystified and then alarmed the fishermen on the "Lucky Dragon" is shown as a flying allegorical monster. Its wings and claws are the weapons of what might one day be universal disaster. It is therefore infinitely more baleful than the animal Shahn had used in the Hickman series to symbolize the tragic yet local fury of a household fire. Today, of course, the whole world is threatened by the ashes of an uncontrollable, celestial blaze. The dilemma of mankind is pungently dramatized in two other paintings from the "Lucky Dragon" series: "I Never Dared to Dream" and "Farewell" (plates 97, 92) and both pictures reaffirm the artist's expressive mastery in depicting the gesticulations of the human hand.

WHEREAS SHAHN'S early career abounded in rebuffs and disappointments, today his art in all its media and forms is in great demand. Collectors and curators eagerly await his newest paintings and drawings; business firms besiege him to work on commissioned assignments. The rise to renown has left him stubbornly unchanged. His words in Selden

29

Rodman's *Portrait of the Artist as an American* (1951) still hold true: "I'm sadly dulled to fame, too, now that it has come at last, because during all those years of obscurity I protected myself with the philosophy that a headful of thoughts and a roomful of paintings were the important things in life even if the public never found out about either. I still think so."

REPRODUCTIONS OF PAINTINGS

רַבִּי יוֹסֵי הַגְּלִילִי אוֹמֵר מִנַּיִן אַתָּה
אוֹמֵר שֶׁלָּקוּ הַמִּצְרִיִּים בְּמִצְרַיִם עֶשֶׂ
ר מַכּוֹת. וְעַל הַיָּם לָקוּ חֲמִשִּׁים מַ
כּוֹת. בְּמִצְרַיִם מַה הוּא אוֹמֵר וַיֹּאמְ
רוּ הַחַרְטֻמִּים ֿ פַּרְעֹה אֶצְבַּע אֱלֹהִים
הוּא: וְעַל הַיָּם מַה הוּא אוֹמֵר וַיַּרְ
ְא יִשְׂרָאֵל אֶת הַיָּד הַגְּדֹלָה אֲ
שֶׁר עָשָׂה יי בְּמִצְרַיִם וַיִּירְאוּ הָ
עָם אֶת יי וַיַּאֲמִינוּ בַּיי וּבְמֹשֶׁה
עַבְדּוֹ ֿ כַּמָּה לָקוּ בְּאֶצְבַּע עֶשֶׂר
מַכּוֹת ֿ אֱמוֹר מֵעַתָּה בְּמִצְרַיִם לָקוּ
עֶשֶׂר מַכּוֹת ֿ וְעַל הַיָּם לָקוּ חֲמִשִּׁים
מַכּוֹת:
רַבִּי אֱלִיעֶזֶר אוֹמֵר מִנַּיִן שֶׁכָּל
מַכָּה וּמַכָּה שֶׁהֵבִיא הַקָּדוֹשׁ בָּרוּךְ
הוּא עַל הַמִּצְרִיִּים בְּמִצְרַיִם הָיְתָה
שֶׁל אַרְבַּע מַכּוֹת ֿ שֶׁנֶּאֱמַר יְשַׁלַּח
בָּם חֲרוֹן אַפּוֹ עֶבְרָה וָזַעַם וְצָרָה
מִשְׁלַחַת מַלְאֲכֵי רָעִים ֿ עֶבְרָה
וָזַעַם שְׁתַּיִם ֿ וְצָרָה שָׁלֹשׁ
מִשְׁלַחַת מַלְאֲכֵי רָעִים אַרְבַּע ֿ אֱמוֹר
מֵעַתָּה בְּמִצְרַיִם לָקוּ אַרְבָּעִים מַכּוֹת
וְעַל הַיָּם לָקוּ מָאתַיִם מַכּוֹת:
רַבִּי עֲקִיבָא אוֹמֵר ֿ מִנַּיִן שֶׁכָּל מַ
כָּה וּמַכָּה שֶׁהֵבִיא הַקָּדוֹשׁ בָּרוּךְ
הוּא עַל הַמִּצְרִיִּים בְּמִצְרַיִם הָיְתָה
שֶׁל חָמֵשׁ מַכּוֹת ֿ שֶׁנֶּאֱמַר יְשַׁלַּח בָּ
ם חֲרוֹן אַפּוֹ עֶבְרָה וָזַעַם וְצָרָה מִשְׁ
לַחַת מַלְאֲכֵי רָעִים ֿ חֲרוֹן אַפּוֹ אַחַת

2   *Demonstration in Paris • 1932 • Collection, Mr. Elmer Rice*

3    *Bartolomeo Vanzetti and Nicola Sacco and their guards • 1932 • Collection, Miss Patricia Healey*

4   *Tom Mooney with his mother and his wife* • *1933* • *Collection, Mr. and Mrs. Herbert Goldstone*

5    *Tom Mooney and his warden, J.B. Holohan* • *1933* • *Owned by the artist*

6   *Double self-portrait • 1933 • Courtesy, The Downtown Gallery*

7   *W.C.T.U. parade • 1933-34 • Museum of the City of New York*

8    *Scott's run, West Virginia • 1937 • The Whitney Museum of American Art*

9    *Sunday painting • 1938 • Collection, Mrs. Ben Shahn*

10   *Sunday football • 1938 • Estate of Mr. Herman Shulman*

11    *Fresco mural in the Community Center of the Federal Housing Development, Roosevelt, New Jersey • 1937-38*

12 *Poster for the C.I.O. • 1946 • The Museum of Modern Art, New York (Gift of Mrs. S. S. Spivack)*

13    *World's greatest comics • 1946 • Collection, Mrs. Edith Gregor Halpert*

14    *Textile mills • 1938-39 • Fresco in the Bronx Central Annex Post Office, New York*

15   *Picking cotton • 1938-39 • Fresco in the Bronx Central Annex Post Office, New York*

16 *Seurat's lunch • 1939 • Collection, Mr. and Mrs. Earle Ludgin*

17   *Photographer's window* • *1939* • *Collection, Mr. and Mrs. Lawrence Richmond*

18   *Contemporary American sculpture* • *1939* • *Collection, Joseph Kaufman*

19    *Vacant lot • 1939 • Wadsworth Atheneum, Ella Gallup Sumner and Mary Catlin Sumner Collection*

20   *Handball • 1939 • The Museum of Modern Art, New York (Mrs. John D. Rockefeller, Jr., Fund)*

21   *Portion of fresco mural in the Federal Security Building, Washington, D.C.* • *1940-42*

22    *Portion of fresco mural in the Federal Security Building, Washington, D.C.* • *1940-42*

23  *Willis Avenue bridge • 1940 • The Museum of Modern Art, New York (Gift of Lincoln Kirstein)*

24    *Four piece orchestra • 1944 • Collection, S. J. Perelman*

25  *Pretty girl milking a cow • 1940 • Collection, Edgar Kaufmann, Jr.*

26  *Sunday morning • 1943 • Collection, University of Georgia*

27   *French workers • 1942 • Courtesy  The Downtown Gallery*

28  *Girl jumping rope • 1943 • Collection, Mr. and Mrs. Stephen Stone*

29    *Spring • 1946 • Room of Contemporary Art Collection, Albright-Knox Art Gallery*

30    *Fourth-of-July orator • 1943 • Collection, Mr. James Thrall Soby*

31    *Peter and the wolf* • 1943 • *Collection, Mrs. Eero Saarinen*

32   *Italian landscape, I • 1944 • Walker Art Center*

33   *Italian landscape, II • 1944 • Collection, Mr. and Mrs. Irving Levick*

34   *Cherubs and children • 1944 • The Whitney Museum of American Art*

35    *The red stairway* • *1944* • *City Art Museum of St. Louis*

for full employment after the war
REGISTER • VOTE
CIO POLITICAL ACTION COMMITTEE

36    *Employment poster for the C.I.O.* • *1944* • *The Museum of Modern Art, New York*

37   Reconstruction • 1945 • The Whitney Museum of American Art

38   *Liberation • 1945 • Collection, Mr. James Thrall Soby*

39   *Brothers • 1946 • Courtesy, The Joseph H. Hirshhorn Foundation, Inc.*

40    *Nearly everybody reads the* Bulletin • *1946* • *Louis E. Stern Estate, on loan to The Brooklyn Museum*

41   *Nocturne • 1949 • Willard Straight Hall (Student Union), Cornell University*

42  *The violin player • 1947 • The Museum of Modern Art, New York (Sam A. Lewisohn Bequest)*

43   *Trouble • 1947 • F. M. Hall Collection, University of Nebraska*

44    *East 12th Street* • *1947* • *Collection, Mr. and Mrs. Albert Hackett*

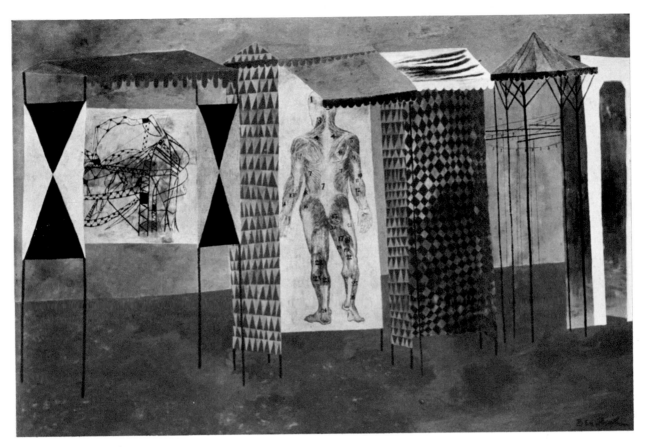

45   *The anatomical man • 1949 • Collection, Miss Mary E. Johnston*

46   *Interior • 1948 • Collection, Mr. and Mrs. Walter Paepcke*

47   *Silent music* • *1948* • *Phillips Collection*

48 *Allegory • 1948 • Collection, Bill Bomar*

49  *Convention • 1949 • Collection, Mr. and Mrs. George W. W. Brewster*

50   Epoch • 1950 • *The Philadelphia Museum of Art*

51 *On the first day of Christmas* • *1949* • *Collection, Mr. Jack Zungmeyer*

52  *Labyrinth • 1952 • Collection, Mr. and Mrs. George W. W. Brewster*

*53   Ave • 1950 • Wadsworth Atheneum*

54  *Second allegory • 1952 • Krannert Art Museum
University of Illinois*

55  *Maimonides • 1954 • Collection, Mr. and Mrs. John Rood*

55A.   *Maimonides (Detail)*

56   *Anger • 1952 • Collection, Mrs. Edith Gregor Halpert*

57   *City of dreadful night* • *1951* • *Collection, Mr. and Mrs. Robert F. Windfor*

58   *Incubus • 1954 • Collection, Mr. and Mrs. Emmons R. Bahan*

59    *The defaced portrait • 1955 • Collection, Mr. and Mrs. Hoke Levin*

60  *Byzantine isometric • 1951 • Collection, Mr. and Mrs. Stanley Wolf*

61    *Composition with clarinets and tin horn* • *1951* • *The Detroit Institute of Arts*

62   *Third allegory • 1955 • Collection, Mr. and Mrs. Irving Levick*

63   Harpie • 1951 • Collection, Mr. Robert Mayer

64   *Age of anxiety • 1953 • Courtesy, The Joseph H. Hirshhorn Foundation, Inc.*

65   *Everyman* • *1954* • *The Whitney Museum of American Art*

66    *Second spring • 1955 • Collection, Mr. and Mrs. John Barclay*

67   *Goyescas • 1956 • Collection, Mr. Paul Roebling*

68   *Chicago • 1955 • Collection, Dr. and Mrs. Michael Watter*

69   *Blind botanist • 1954 • Roland P. Murdock Collection, The Wichita Art Museum*

70   *Folk song • 1956 • Collection, Armand Erpf*

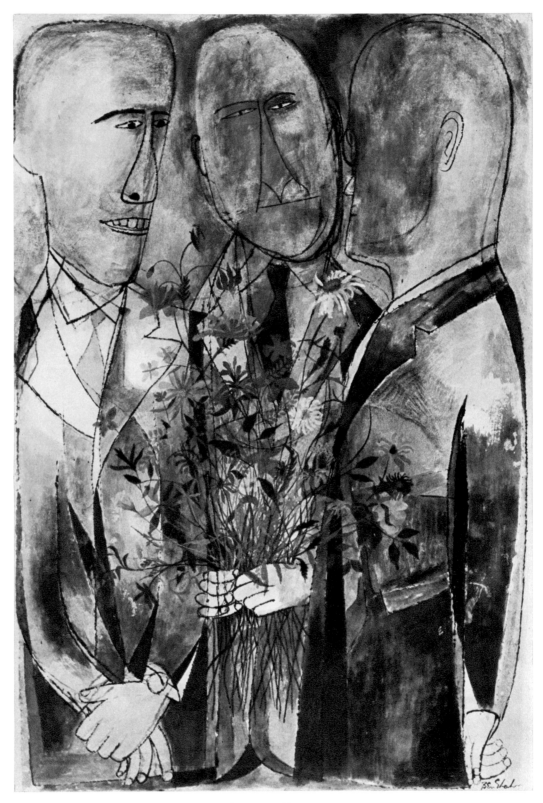

71   Cosmos • 1957 • Collection, Mr. and Mrs. Jacob Kaplan

72  *Pacific landscape* • 1945 • *The Museum of Modern Art, New York* (*Gift of Philip L. Goodwin*)

73  *Song* • 1950 • *Courtesy, The Joseph H. Hirshhorn Foundation, Inc.*

74   *Vulture • 1961 • Collection, Mrs. Ben Shahn*

75    *Portrait of Dag Hammarskjold • 1962 • Courtesy, Nationalmuseum, Stockholm*

BEHOLD, HOW GOOD AND HOW PLEASANT IT IS FOR BRETHREN TO DWELL TOGETHER IN UNITY!
IT IS LIKE
THE PRECIOUS
OINTMENT
UPON THE HEAD...
AS THE DEW
OF HERMON
AND AS THE DEW
THAT DESCENDED
UPON THE MOUNTAINS
OF ZION:
FOR THERE THE LORD
COMMANDED
THE BLESSING,
EVEN LIFE
FOR EVERMORE.

77    *Helix and crystal • 1957 • Collection, Mr. and Mrs. Joseph Strick*

78   *Third alphabet* • 1957 • *Collection, Mr. and Mrs. Walter Werner*

79    *When the saints . . . • 1956 • Collection, Mr. and Mrs. Fred W. Friendly*

80   *Lute, I • 1957 • Collection, Mrs. L. B. Wescott*

81    *Ram's horn and Menorah • 1958 • Collection, Mr. and Mrs. Jacob Schulman*

82   *Lute and molecules • 1958 • Collection, Mr. and Mrs. A. Leon Fergenson*

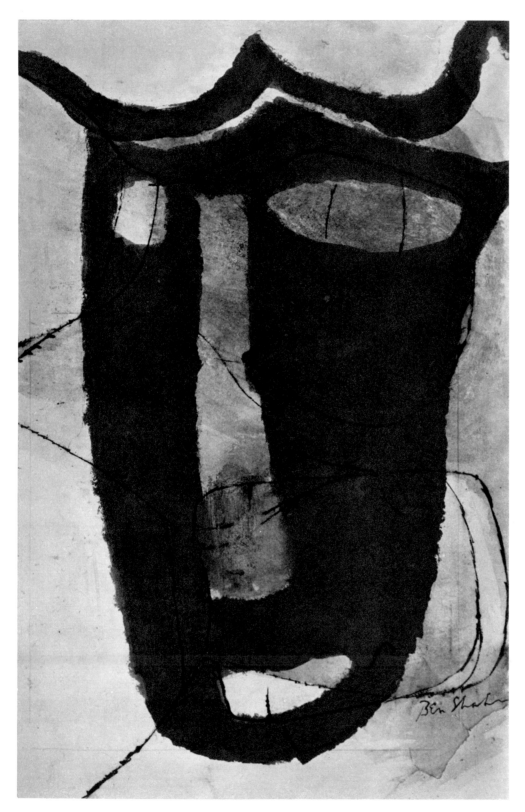

83   *Mask of the devil (or JB's blue Satan) 1958*
*Courtesy, Fogg Art Museum, Harvard University*

84   *Parable • 1958 • Munson-Williams-Proctor Institute*

85    *A childhood memory • 1962 • Courtesy, The Downtown Gallery*

86   *Still life with Persian vase* • *1959* • *Collection, Mr. and Mrs. Gregory Stainow*

87 *Conversations • 1958*
*The Whitney Museum of American Art*
*(Gift of the Friends of The Whitney Museum of American Art)*

88  *The physicist ("Lucky Dragon" series) • 1961*
*Collection, Mr. Jack Lawrence and The Lawrence-Myden Foundation*

I AM A FISHERMAN
AIKICHI KUBOYAMA
BY NAME. ON THE
FIRST OF MARCH
1954 OUR FISHING
BOAT THE LUCKY
DRAGON WANDERED
UNDER AN ATOMIC CLOUD
EIGHTY MILES FROM
BIKINI. I AND MY FRIENDS
WERE BURNED.
WE DID NOT KNOW
WHAT HAPPENED TO US.
ON SEPTEMBER TWENTY
THIRD OF THAT YEAR
I DIED OF ATOMIC BURN.

89 *The Lucky Dragon ("Lucky Dragon" series) • 1960 • Courtesy, The Downtown Gallery*

90 *From that day on ("Lucky Dragon" series) • 1961 • Collection, James Michener*

91   Why ("*Lucky Dragon*" series) • *1961* • *Collection, Mr. and Mrs. Herbert Goldstone*

92  *Farewell ("Lucky Dragon" series) • 1961 • Collection, Mrs. Edith Gregor Halpert*

93 *A score of white pigeons ("Lucky Dragon" series) • 1961 • Courtesy, Nationalmuseum, Stockholm*

94  *We did not know what happened to us (''Lucky Dragon'' series) • 1960*
    *''Art; U.S.A.; Now'' Collection, S. C. Johnson and Son, Inc.*

95   *That Friday: Yaizu ("Lucky Dragon" series)* • *1961* • *Courtesy, The Downtown Gallery*

96   *Kuboyama ("Lucky Dragon" series)* • *1961* • *Collection, Robert Straus*

97   *I never dared to dream ("Lucky Dragon" series)* • *1960* • *Collection, The Norton Gallery*

98   *It's no use to do any more ("Lucky Dragon" series)* • 1961-62 • Courtesy, The Downtown Gallery

*Indicates color plate.*
*Dimensions are given in inches;*
*height precedes width.*

**LIST OF PLATES**

Endpapers: *Detail of plate 51.*

129

•12 We want peace, register, vote. *(Poster for C. I. O.) 1946. Lithograph, 41½ x 27. The Museum of Modern Art, New York (Gift of Mrs. S. S. Spivack)*

•13 World's greatest comics. *1946. Tempera, 35 x 48. Collection, Mrs. Edith Gregor Halpert*

14 Textile mills. *Fresco panel in the Bronx Central Annex Post Office, New York, 1938-39. Photo Moyer*

15 Picking cotton. *Fresco panel in the Bronx Central Annex Post Office, New York. 1938-39. Photo Moyer*

16 Seurat's lunch. *1939. Tempera, 20 x 30. Collection, Mr. and Mrs. Earle Ludgin*

17 Photographer's window. *1939. Tempera, 22½ x 31. Collection, Mr. and Mrs. Lawrence Richmond. Photo Colten*

18 Contemporary American sculpture. *1939. Tempera, 24½ x 33. Collection, Joseph Kaufman*

19 Vacant lot. *1939. Tempera, 19 x 23. Collection, Ella Gallup Sumner and Mary Catlin Sumner, Wadsworth Atheneum, Hartford, Connecticut*

20 Handball. *1939. Tempera, 22¾ x 33¼. The Museum of Modern Art, New York (Mrs. John D. Rockefeller, Jr., Fund). Photo Soichi Sunami*

21 Portion of fresco mural in the Federal Security Building, *Washington, D.C., 1940-42*

22 Portion of fresco mural in the Federal Security Building, *Washington, D.C., 1940-42*

23 Willis Avenue bridge. *1940. Tempera, 23 x 31⅜. The Museum of Modern Art, New York (Gift of Lincoln Kirstein)*

•24 Four piece orchestra. *1944. Tempera, 18 x 24. Collection, S. J. Perelman*

25 Pretty girl milking a cow. *1940. Tempera, 22 x 30. Collection, Edgar Kaufman, Jr.*

26 Sunday morning. *1943. Tempera, 16 x 24. Collection, University of Georgia, Athens, Georgia*

27 French workers. *1942. Tempera, 40 x 57. Courtesy, The Downtown Gallery, New York. Photo O. E. Nelson*

28 Girl jumping rope. *1943. Tempera, 16 x 24. Collection, Mr. and Mrs. Stephen Stone*

•29 Spring. *1946. Tempera, 17 x 30. Room of Contemporary Art Collection, Albright-Knox Art Gallery, Buffalo, New York*

30 Fourth of July orator. *1943. Tempera, 22 x 30. Collection, Mr. James Thrall Soby*

31 Peter and the wolf. *1943. Tempera, 6½ x 10. Collection, Mrs. Eero Saarinen*

32  Italian landscape, I. *1944. Tempera, 28 x 36. Walker Art Center, Minneapolis, Minnesota*

• 33  Italian landscape, II. *1944. Tempera, 27½ x 30½. Collection, Mr. and Mrs. Irving Levick. Photo Sherwin Greenberg*

34  Cherubs and children. *1944. Tempera, 15½ x 23½. The Whitney Museum of American Art, New York*

35  The red stairway. *1944. Tempera, 16 x 23½. City Art Museum of St. Louis, Missouri*

• 36  For full employment after the war register, vote *(Poster for the C. I. O.). 1944. Lithograph, 30 x 39⅞. The Museum of Modern Art, New York*

37  Reconstruction. *1945. Tempera, 26 x 39. The Whitney Museum of American Art, New York. Photo Colten*

38  Liberation. *1945. Tempera, 30 x 39½. Collection, Mr. James Thrall Soby. Photo Oliver Baker*

39  Brothers. *1946. Tempera, 39 x 26. Courtesy, The Joseph H. Hirshhorn Foundation, Inc. New York. Photo W. Rosenblum*

40  Nearly everybody reads the *Bulletin. 1946. Tempera, 22 x 30. Louis E. Stern Estate, on loan to The Brooklyn Museum, New York. Photo Oliver Baker*

• 41  Nocturne. *1949. Tempera, 40 x 27. Willard Straight Hall (Student Union) Cornell University*

42  The violin player. *1947. Tempera, 40 x 26. The Museum of Modern Art, New York (Sam A. Lewisohn Bequest). Photo Oliver Baker*

43  Trouble. *1947. Tempera, 24 x 36. F. M. Hall Collection, University of Nebraska, Lincoln, Nebraska. Photo Oliver Baker*

44  East 12th Street. *1947. Tempera, 27 x 40. Collection, Mr. and Mrs. Albert Hackett. Photo Oliver Baker*

• 45  The anatomical man. *1949. Tempera, 27 x 40. Collection, Miss Mary E. Johnson*

46  Interior. *1948. Tempera, 40 x 27. Collection, Mr. and Mrs. Walter Paepcke. Photo Oliver Baker*

47  Silent music. *1948. Tempera, 48 x 83½. Phillips Collection, Washington, D.C. Photo Oliver Baker*

48  Allegory. *1948. Tempera, 36 x 48. Collection, Bill Somar. Photo Oliver Baker*

• 49  Convention. *1949. Tempera, 30 x 46. Collection, Mr. and Mrs. George W. W. Brewster*

50  Epoch. *1950. Tempera, 52 x 31. The Philadelphia Museum of Art, Philadelphia, Pennsylvania. Photo Oliver Baker*

51  On the first day of Christmas. *1949. Tempera, 35¼ x 23¾. Collection, Mr. Jack Zungmeyer. Photo Oliver Baker*

52 Labyrinth. *1952. Tempera, 47½ x 35½. Collection, Mr. and Mrs. George W. W. Brewster. Photo Oliver Baker*

• 53 Ave, *1950. Tempera, 31 x 52. Wadsworth Atheneum, Hartford, Connecticut*

54 Second allegory. *1952. Tempera, 52 x 30¾. Krannert Art Museum, University of Illinois, Urbana, Illinois, Photo Oliver Baker*

55 Maimonides. *1954. Watercolor, 34 x 26. Collection, Mr. and Mrs. John Rood. Photo Oliver Baker*

55A Maimonides (Detail). *Photo Oliver Baker*

56 Anger. *1952. Gouache, 39 x 25¼. Collection, Mrs. Edith Gregor Halpert. Photo Oliver Baker*

• 57 City of dreadful night. *1951. Tempera, 47½ x 56. Collection, Mr. and Mrs. Robert F. Windfor*

58 Incubus. *1954. Watercolor, 52 x 26. Collection, Mr. and Mrs. Emmons R. Bahan. Photo Oliver Baker*

59 The defaced portrait. *1955. Tempera, 40 x 27. Collection, Mr. and Mrs. Hoke Levin. Photo Oliver Baker*

• 60 Byzantine isometric. *1951. Tempera, 39¼ x 25¾. Collection, Mr. and Mrs. Stanley Wolf*

• 61 Composition with clarinets and tin horn. *1951. Tempera, 48 x 36. The Detroit Institute of Arts, Detroit, Michigan*

62 Third allegory. *1955. Watercolor, 40 x 27. Collection, Mr. and Mrs. Irving Levick*

63 Harpie. *1951. Gouache, 25½ x 33. Collection, Mr. Robert Mayer. Photo Oliver Baker*

• 64 Age of Anxiety. *1953. Tempera, 31 x 52. Courtesy, The Joseph H. Hirshhorn Foundation, Inc., New York.*

• 65 Everyman. *1954. Tempera, 72 x 54. The Whitney Museum of American Art, New York*

66 Second spring. *1955. Tempera, 52 x 32. Private collection. Photo P. A. Juley*

67 Goyescas. *1956. Watercolor, 39 x 26½. Collection, Mr. Paul Roebling. Photo Oliver Baker*

• 68 Chicago. *1955. Watercolor, 36 x 50. Collection, Dr. and Mrs. Michael Watter*

• 69 Blind botanist. *1954. Tempera, 52 x 31. Roland P. Murdock Collection, The Wichita Art Museum, Wichita, Kansas*

70 Folk song. *1956. Watercolor and gouache, 31 x 22½. Collection, Armand Erpf. Photo Oliver Baker*

71 Cosmos. *1957. Watercolor, 39 x 26. Collection, Mr. and Mrs. Jacob Kaplan. Photo Oliver Baker*

•72 Pacific landscape. *1945. Tempera, 25½ x 39. The Museum of Modern Art, New York (Gift of Philip L. Goodwin)*

•73 Song. *1950. Tempera, 52 x 31. Courtesy, The Joseph H. Hirshhorn Foundation, Inc., New York*

74 Vulture. *1961. Watercolor and ink. Collection, Mrs. Ben Shahn. Photo R. Burckhardt*

•75 Portrait of Dag Hammarskjold. *1962. Tempera, 59½ x 47¾. Courtesy, Nationalmuseum, Stockholm*

76 Alternatives. *1962. Tempera and gold leaf, 24 x 53. Courtesy, The Downtown Gallery, New York. Photo O. E. Nelson*

77 Helix and crystal. *1957. Tempera, 53 x 30. Collection, Mr. and Mrs. Joseph Strick. Photo Oliver Baker*

78 Third alphabet. *1957. Drawing, 40¼ x 27. Collection, Mr. and Mrs. Walter Werner. Photo Oliver Baker*

79 When the saints . . . *1956. Tempera, 53 x 30. Collection, Mr. and Mrs. Fred W. Friendly. Photo Oliver Baker*

80 Lute, I. *1957. Gouache, 25½ x 39. Collection, Mrs. L. B. Wescott. Photo Oliver Baker*

81 Ram's horn and menorah. *1958. Tempera, 16 x 27¼. Collection, Mr. and Mrs. Jacob Schulman. Photo Oliver Baker*

82 Lute and molecules. *1958. Gouache, 27 x 40½. Collection, Mr. and Mrs. A. Leon Fergenson. Photo Oliver Baker*

83 Mask of the devil (or JB's blue satan). *1958. Watercolor, 23 x 14¾. Courtesy, Fogg Art Museum, Harvard University, Cambridge, Massachusetts. Photo Oliver Baker*

•84 Parable. *1958. Tempera, 48 x 38. Munson-Williams-Proctor Institute, Utica, New York*

85 A childhood memory. *1962. Watercolor and gouache, 18 x 18. Courtesy, The Downtown Gallery, New York. Photo O. E. Nelson*

86 Still life with Persian vase. *1959. Watercolor, 26 x 19½. Collection, Mr. and Mrs. Gregory Stainow. Photo Oliver Baker*

•87 Conversations. *1958. Watercolor, 36¾ x 25½. The Whitney Museum of American Art, New York (Gift of the Friends of the Whitney Museum of American Art)*

88 The physicist ("Lucky Dragon" series). *1961. Tempera, 52 x 31. Collection, Mr. Jack Lawrence and The Lawrence-Myden Foundation. Photo Oliver Baker*

89 The Lucky Dragon *("Lucky Dragon" series). 1960. Tempera, 84 x 48. Courtesy, The Downtown Gallery, New York. Photo Oliver Baker*

90 From that day on *("Lucky Dragon" series). 1961. Tempera, 72 x 36. Collection James Michener. Photo Oliver Baker*

91 Why *("Lucky Dragon" series). 1961. Gouache, 20 x 26. Collection, Mr. and Mrs. Herbert Goldtone. Photo O. E. Nelson*

92 Farewell *("Lucky Dragon" series). 1961. Gouache, 23 x 31. Collection, Mrs. Edith Gregor Halpert. Photo Oliver Baker*

93 A score of white pigeons *("Lucky Dragon" series). 1961. Tempera, 48 x 30. Courtesy, Nationalmuseum, Stockholm. Photo Oliver Baker*

94 We did not know what happened to us *("Lucky Dragon" series). 1960. Tempera, 48 x 72. "Art; U.S.A.; Now" Collection, S. C. Johnson and Son, Inc., Racine, Wisconsin. Photo Oliver Baker*

95 That Friday: Yaizu *("Lucky Dragon" series). 1961. Gouache, 16¾ x 50¼. Courtesy, The Downtown Gallery, New York. Photo Oliver Baker*

96 Kuboyama *("Lucky Dragon" series). 1961. Painting in ink, 25½ x 39. Collection, Robert Straus. Photo O. E. Nelson*

• 97 I never dared to dream *("Lucky Dragon" series). 1960. Gouache, 27 x 40. Collection, The Norton Gallery, West Palm Beach, Florida*

98 It's no use to do any more *("Lucky Dragon" series). 1961-62. Tempera, 25½ x 39. Courtesy, The Downtown Gallery, New York. Photo Oliver Baker*

## CHRONOLOGY

1898  Born Kovno, Lithuania.

1906  To America. Lived with his family in Brooklyn, New York.

1913–17  Employed as lithographer's apprentice during day, attended high school at night. (Employed as a lithographer off and on until 1930.)

1919–22  Attended New York University and later City College of New York. Summer scholarship at Marine Biological Laboratory, Woods Hole, Massachusetts. Left City College in 1922 to study at National Academy of Design.

1925  Travel abroad: France, Italy, Spain, North Africa.

1927  Second trip to Europe and North Africa. Influenced by school of Paris masters, especially Rouault and Dufy.

1929–30  Returned to America, 1929. First one-man show at The Downtown Gallery, New York, April 8–27, 1930: watercolors and drawings of African subjects; three studio compositions in oil. Painted at Truro, Massachusetts, mainly beach scenes.

1931–32  Beginning of mature career with 23 small gouache paintings and two large panels on the Sacco-Vanzetti case. Shown at The Downtown Gallery and the Harvard Society for Contemporary Art, 1932. The two large panels exhibited at The Museum of Modern Art, New York.

1932–33  Completed 15 gouache paintings and a tempera panel on the case of labor leader Tom Mooney. These admired by Mexican artist Diego Rivera, who hired Shahn as his assistant in painting ill-fated fresco, "Man at the Crossroads," for RCA Building in Rockefeller Center, New York.

135

**1933-34** Enrolled with Public Works of Art Project. For New York City office of Project painted series of 8 small tempera pictures on Prohibition Era, for a projected but never executed mural decoration in Central Park Casino.

**1934** With artist Lou Block commissioned by the Federal Emergency Relief Administration to prepare murals for a prison corridor at Riker's Island Penitentiary, New York.

**1935** His sketches for these murals rejected by the Municipal Art Commission, though previously approved by Mayor and Commissioner of Correction.

**1935-38** Employed by the Farm Security Administration as artist, designer, and, briefly, photographer. Exhibition, December 1936 at WPA Federal Art Project Gallery, New York, of Documentary Photographs from Files of the Resettlement Administration including photographs by Shahn, Walker Evans, Arnold Rothstein, Dorothea Lange, T. Jung, Carl Mydans, E. Johnson, P. Carter.

**1937-38** Completed for Farm Security Administration fresco for community center of a federal housing development at Roosevelt, New Jersey. (Shahn himself lives in this development.) Easel paintings.

**1938-39** Shahn and his wife, Bernarda Bryson, commissioned by the Section of Fine Arts, Public Buildings Administration, U.S. Treasury, to paint 13 large fresco panels for the main lobby of Bronx Central Annex Post Office, New York. Work completed August 1939.

**1939-40** Completed for the same federal agency 9 scale sketches for projected series of murals on the Four Freedoms, intended for the post office at St. Louis, Missouri. Sketches rejected and project awarded to other artists. In 1939 painted for Section of Fine Arts an over-door panel on canvas for Jamaica, Long Island, post office. Many easel paintings. One-man show at Julien Levy Gallery, New York, May 1940.

**1940-42** Entered and won competition with 375 artists for Section of Fine Arts' commission for murals for main corridor of Federal Security Building, Washington, D.C.

**1942-43** Designed posters for Office of War Information. Only two of his posters published.

**1943-present** Many commercial commissions for Container Corporation of America, Columbia Broadcasting System, Columbia Records, *Fortune, Time, Charm, Seventeen, Esquire, Harper's, Scientific American,* Vintage Books, among others.

**1943-44** Easel paintings. Five posters for Political Action Committee of the C.I.O. Represented by 11 paintings in exhibition, "American Realists and Magic Realists," The Museum of Modern Art, New York, 1943. 1944: One-man show at The Downtown Gallery, New York.

**1945-46** Director of graphic arts division of the C.I.O. Four posters for this organization. Easel paintings. 1946: Included in exhibition of American painting at the Tate Gallery, London.

136

1947 Taught at Boston Museum Summer School, Pittsfield, Massachusetts. Monograph on his work in Penguin Modern Painters series, London and New York. Retrospective exhibition of 10 paintings, Mayor Gallery, London, under auspices of Arts Council of Great Britain. Retrospective exhibition of paintings, drawings, posters, illustrations, and photographs at The Museum of Modern Art, New York, September 30, 1947–January 4, 1948.

1948 Selected one of Ten Best Painters in poll by *Look* magazine. Designed posters and campaign material for Henry Wallace's Third Party movement.

1949 One-man show at The Downtown Gallery, New York, October 25–November 12.

1950 Taught for ten weeks at University of Colorado Summer Session, Boulder, Colorado. One-man shows at Albright Art School, Buffalo, March 17–April 27; at Frank Perls Gallery, Los Angeles; at Phillips Memorial Gallery, Washington, D.C., November 19–December 12.

1951 Taught at Brooklyn Museum Art School. One-man show of drawings at The Downtown Gallery, May 22–June 8; group show (with Willem de Kooning and Jackson Pollock) at Arts Club of Chicago, October 2–27.

1952 Attended and made drawings of Democratic Convention in Chicago. One-man shows at The Downtown Gallery, New York, and Boris Mirsky Gallery, Boston. Group show (with Lee Gatch and Karl Knaths) at Santa Barbara Museum of Art, California Palace of the Legion of Honor, and Los Angeles County Museum.

1953–54 Won $800 award offered by Museum of São Paulo, Brazil. Chosen, with Willem de Kooning to represent American painting at Venice Biennale. One-man show of drawings at Art Institute of Chicago, March 26–April 26.

1955 One-man exhibition at The Downtown Gallery, January 18–February 12, celebrated his 25th year of association with this gallery.

1956 Elected member of the National Institute of Arts and Letters. Won Joseph E. Temple Medal Award at the Pennsylvania Academy. Traveled in Europe.

1956–57 Named Charles Eliot Norton Professor of Poetry at Harvard University. Retrospective exhibition, Fogg Art Museum, Cambridge, Massachusetts, December 4, 1956–January 19, 1957. Completed mosaic for William E. Grady Vocational High School, Brooklyn, New York, commissioned by the New York City Board of Education.

1957 Documentary exhibition surveying separate aspects of Shahn's work, at Institute of Contemporary Art, Boston, Massachusetts.

1958 Designed sets Jerome Robbins' ballet *New York Export–Opus Jazz*, performed at Festival of Two Worlds, Spoleto, Italy. Exhibited "American Artists Paint the City," Venice Biennale. Awarded Institute Medal by American Institute of Graphic Arts.

1959 Exhibition, The Downtown Gallery, and Leicester Galleries, London. Exhibition, Katonah Gallery, Katonah, New York. Won Annual Award, North Shore Art Festival, Long Island. Elected member American Academy of Arts and Sciences. Mosaic for Congregation Oheb Shalom, Nashville, Tennessee. Trip to Far East.

1960 Exhibition of silk screens, University of Louisville. Graphics exhibition, University of Utah. Mosaic for Congregation Mishkan Israel, New Haven, Connecticut. Began work "Lucky Dragon" series.

1961-62 Retrospective Exhibition, organized by International Council of The Museum of Modern Art, New York, circulated: Stedelijk Museum, Amsterdam; Palais des Beaux-Arts, Brussels; Galleria Nazionale d'Arte Moderna, Rome; Albertina, Vienna.

1961 Exhibition, New Haven Jewish Community Center, New Haven, Connecticut. Sets for e.e. cummings' play, *Images*, and for Jerome Robbins' ballet, *Events*, performed at Festival of Two Worlds, Spoleto, Italy. Exhibition, "The Saga of the Lucky Dragon," The Downtown Gallery.

1962 Graphics Exhibition, Armand's Gallery, Sarasota, Florida. Mural for Lemoyne College, Memphis, Tennessee. Posters for Lincoln Center for the Performing Arts, New York and Boston Arts Festival, Boston, Massachusetts.

1962-63 Graphics Exhibition circulated by International Council of The Museum of Modern Art, New York, opened at Staatliche Kunsthalle, Baden-Baden, August '62. Closed in Japan October '63.

*Entries*
*are listed chronologically*
*within each division.*

## BIBLIOGRAPHY

*Writings and statements by Shahn*

Correspondence concerning the Riker's Island murals. New York, 1933-36. (A collection of original letters from Lou Block and Shahn to the commissioning agencies, in the Museum of Modern Art Library, New York.)

MILLER, DOROTHY C. and BARR, ALFRED H., JR. (eds.). *American Realists and Magic Realists.* New York: The Museum of Modern Art, 1943. (Catalogue of exhibition, statement by Shahn, pp. 52-53.)

MORSE, JOHN D. "Ben Shahn: An Interview," *Magazine of Art,* April 1944, pp. 136-41.

MORSE, JOHN D. "Henri Cartier-Bresson," *Magazine of Art,* May 1947, p. 189. (Shahn's opinions on the photographer and on photography in general.)

"An Artist's Credo," *College Art Journal,* Autumn 1949, pp. 43-45. (Condensation of paper read at the Second Annual Art Conference, Woodstock, New York, August 28-29, 1948.)

"The Artist's Point of View," *Magazine of Art,* November 1949, pp. 266, 269. (Text of paper presented at the Seventh Annual Conference on Art Education sponsored by the Museum of Modern Art, New York, March 18-20, 1949. Balcomb Greene, Robert Motherwell, and Shahn participated in the session, The Artist's Point of View.)

"Aspects of the Art of Paul Klee," *Museum of Modern Art Bulletin,* Summer 1950, pp. 6-9. (Speech delivered at the first of a series of symposia presented by the Junior Council of the Museum of Modern Art, New York.)

*Symposium: The Relation of Painting and Sculpture to Architecture.*
New York: The Museum of Modern Art, 1951. (Typescript of symposium, in the Museum of Modern Art Library; includes remarks by Shahn. Published report in *Interiors*, May 1951, p. 102.)

*Paragraphs on Art.* New York: The Spiral Press, 1952. ("The second in a series of brief personal credos prepared at the request of The Spiral Press. These Paragraphs by Ben Shahn gathered from speeches made at various times and places over the past few years ....")

RODMAN, SELDEN (ed.). "Ben Shahn Speaking," *Perspectives USA*, January 1952, pp. 59-72.

"... The Future of the Creative Arts: A Symposium ...," *University of Buffalo Studies*, February 1952, pp. 125-28. (One of several symposia on the theme "The Outlook for Mankind in the Next Half-Century," at the Niagara Frontier Convocation, December 7-8, 1951. Includes text by Shahn; remarks reprinted in Alfred H. Barr, Jr. (ed.), *Masters of Modern Art*, New York: The Museum of Modern Art, 1954, p. 162.)

"What is Realism in Art?," *Look*, January 13, 1953, pp. 44-45.

"The Artist and the Politicians," *Art News*, September 1953, pp. 34-35, 67.

"How an Artist Looks at Aesthetics," *Journal of Aesthetics and Art Criticism*, September 1954, pp. 46-51. (Paper presented at the annual meeting of the American Society for Aesthetics, East Lansing, Michigan, November 20, 1953.)

"They Can Rank with the Greatest Works of Art, But. . . . Famous Painter Asks: Are Cartoons Now Among the Obits?," *Art News*, October 1954, p. 50.

"In the Mail: Art versus Camera," *New York Times*, February 13, 1955, Section 2, p. 15. (A letter to the editor in which Shahn takes exception to the review by Aline B. Saarinen, "The Camera versus the Artist," which discusses the photographic exhibition "The Family of Man" organized by Edward Steichen.)

RODMAN, SELDEN. *Conversations with Artists.* New York: The Devin-Adair Co., 1957. (Interview with Shahn, pp. 189-93, 221-28.)

"Realism Reconsidered," *Perspecta*, 1957, pp. 28-35. (Text of talk given before the Institute of Contemporary Art, London, February 1956, in connection with the Tate Gallery's exhibition, "Modern Art in the United States.")

*The Shape of Content.* Cambridge: Harvard University Press, 1957. (The Charles Eliot Norton lectures of 1956-57. Reprinted New York, 1960, as Vintage Book V-108.)

BRANDON, HENRY. "... A Conversation with Ben Shahn," *New Republic*, July 7, 1958, pp. 15-18. (A taped conversation for the *Sunday Times*, London, which appeared in the March 16, 1958 issue of that newspaper.)

"Shahn in Amsterdam," *Art in America,* Number Three 1961, pp. 62-67. (Shahn presents and interprets a wide selection of his paintings, some of which will be shown in a major retrospective exhibition arranged by the International Council of the Museum of Modern Art, New York.)

"Bill," *The Visual Craft of William Golden,* Cipe Pineles Golden, Kurt Weihs, Robert Strunsky (eds.). New York: George Braziller, 1962, pp. 126-27. (Includes reproductions of work Shahn has done for the Columbia Broadcasting System.)

"In Homage," in "The Talk of the Town," *New Yorker,* September 29, 1962, pp. 31-33. (Interview with Shahn on the memorial dedicated to President Franklin D. Roosevelt, June 2, 1962, in Roosevelt, New Jersey.)

## Monographs and major exhibition catalogues

NEW YORK. THE DOWNTOWN GALLERY. *The Mooney Case by Ben Shahn.* Catalogue of exhibition of 16 gouaches, May 2-20, 1933. Foreword by Diego Rivera.

SOBY, JAMES THRALL. *Ben Shahn* (The Penguin Modern Painters). New York: The Museum of Modern Art and Penguin Books, 1947.

SOBY, JAMES THRALL. "Ben Shahn," *Museum of Modern Art Bulletin,* Summer 1947, pp. 1-47. (Special issue devoted to Shahn retrospective; supplement to the Penguin monograph.)

RODMAN, SELDEN. *Portrait of the Artist as an American. Ben Shahn: A Biography with Pictures.* New York: Harper, 1951.

VENICE. ESPOSIZIONE BIENNALE INTERNAZIONALE D'ARTE XXVII, 1954. STATI UNITI D'AMERICA. *2 Pittori: de Kooning, Shahn . . . . Esposizione organizzata dal Museum of Modern Art, New York.* Catalogue of American section, texts in Italian and English by Andrew Carnduff Ritchie and James Thrall Soby, and statements by the artists.

BOSTON. INSTITUTE OF CONTEMPORARY ART. *Ben Shahn: A Documentary Exhibition.* Mimeographed catalogue of exhibition April 10-May 31, 1957. Foreword by T. M. Messer.

SOBY, JAMES THRALL. *Ben Shahn: His Graphic Art.* New York: George Braziller, 1957.

GOLDEN, CIPE P. *A Medal for Ben.* New York: American Institute of Graphic Arts, 1959. (Remarks delivered by Mrs. Golden at the presentation of the medal of the American Institute of Graphic Arts to Ben Shahn at a dinner meeting in New York, November 13, 1958.)

NEW YORK. THE DOWNTOWN GALLERY. *Ben Shahn: The Saga of the Lucky Dragon.* Catalogue of exhibition of paintings and drawings, October 10-November 4, 1961.

AMSTERDAM. STEDELIJK MUSEUM. *Ben Shahn.* Catalogue of exhibition circulated by the International Council of the Museum of Modern Art, December 22, 1961-January 22, 1962.

BRUSSELS. PALAIS DES BEAUX-ARTS. *Ben Shahn*. Catalogue of exhibition circulated by the International Council of The Museum of Modern Art, February 3-25, 1962.

ROME. GALLERIA NAZIONALE D'ARTE MODERNA. *Ben Shahn*. Catalogue of the exhibition circulated by the International Council of the Museum of Modern Art, March 31-April 29, 1962.

VIENNA. ALBERTINA. *Ben Shahn*. Catalogue of exhibition circulated by the International Council of the Museum of Modern Art, May 22-June 24, 1962.

## General references

SOBY, JAMES THRALL. *Contemporary Painters*. New York: The Museum of Modern Art, 1948, pp. 40-50.

LARKIN, OLIVER. *Art and Life in America*. New York: Rinehart, 1949, pp. 430, 437-38, 441, 465, 466, 476-79.

PEARSON, RALPH M. *The Modern Renaissance in American Art*. New York: Harper, 1954, pp. 117-23.

BAUR, JOHN (ed.). *New Art in America: Fifty Painters of the 20th Century*. Greenwich, Connecticut: New York Graphic Society in co-operation with Frederick A. Praeger, Inc., New York, 1957, "Ben Shahn," by James Thrall Soby, pp. 118-23; statement by the artist, p. 123.

ELIOT, ALEXANDER. *Three Hundred Years of American Painting*. New York: Time, Inc., 1957, pp. 237, 239-41, 242.

VOLLMER, HANS. *Allgemeines Lexikon der bildenden Künstler*. Leipzig, 1958, IV, pp. 268-69.

GOODRICH, LLOYD and BAUR, JOHN. *American Art of Our Century*. New York: Published for the Whitney Museum of American Art by Frederick A. Praeger, Inc., 1961, pp. 101, 158, 163, 165.

## Articles

"Ben Shahn: The Downtown Gallery," *Art News*, April 19, 1932, p. 10. (Review of Sacco-Vanzetti exhibition.)

GUTMAN, WALTER. "The Passion of Sacco-Vanzetti," *The Nation*, April 20, 1932, p. 475. (Review of The Downtown Gallery exhibition.)

JOSEPHSON, MATTHEW. "Passion of Sacco-Vanzetti," *New Republic*, April 20, 1932, p. 275.

"Ben Shahn: The Downtown Gallery," *Art News*, May 13, 1933, p. 5. (Review of Mooney exhibition.)

CHARLOT, JEAN. "Ben Shahn," *Hound and Horn*, July-September 1933, pp. 632-34.

GELLERT, HUGO. "We Captured the Walls!," *Art Front*, November 1934, p. 8. (About the proposed rejection of murals submitted for the Museum of Modern Art exhibition.)

DAVIS, STUART. " 'We Reject'—the Art Commission," *Art Front*, July 1935, pp. 4-5. (Protests the rejection of the Riker's Island mural by the Municipal Art Commission; illustrations of a section and a detail of the proposed mural.)

WHITING, PHILIPPA. "Speaking About Art: Riker's Island," *The American Magazine of Art*, August 1935, pp. 492-96. (About the rejection of sketches by Shahn and Block; includes opinions of the prisoners.)

"The Bronx—A Typical Treasury Competition," *Art Digest*, June 1, 1938, p. 26.

"New Deal Defeatism," *Daily Mirror* (New York), October 16, 1944, p. 17. (Election campaign, anti-Roosevelt editorial using as its starting point Shahn's poster FOR FULL EMPLOYMENT AFTER THE WAR—REGISTER—VOTE.)

CONNOLLY, CYRIL. "An American Tragedy," *New Statesman and Nation*, June 29, 1946, pp. 467-68. (Review of the Tate Gallery exhibition of American art.)

WILENSKI, R. H. "A London Look at U.S. Painting in the Tate Gallery Show," *Art News*, August 1946, pp. 23-29. (Refers to Shahn's *Liberation*.)

ABELL, WALTER. "Art and Labor," *Magazine of Art*, October 1946, pp. 231, 235-36, 239, 254-56. (Discusses Shahn's contributions to the CIO Political Action Committee.)

SOBY, JAMES THRALL. "Ben Shahn and Morris Graves," *Horizon* (London), October 1947, pp. 48-57.

GREENBERG, CLEMENT. "Art" [a column], *The Nation*, November 1, 1947, p. 481. (Review of the Museum of Modern Art retrospective.)

SOBY, JAMES THRALL. "Ben Shahn," *Graphis 22*, 1948, pp. 102-7, 188-89.

HESS, THOMAS B. "Ben Shahn Paints a Picture," *Art News*, May 1949, pp. 20-22, 55-56. (Photographic story by Thelma Martin.)

BRYSON, BERNARDA. "The Drawings of Ben Shahn," *Image* (London), Autumn 1949, pp. 31-50. (Includes reproductions of drawings for the CBS programs *Fear Begins at Forty* and *Mind in the Shadow*, and for articles in the *New Republic, Fortune*, and *Harper's*.)

CHANIN, A. L. "Shahn, Sandburg of the Painters," *The Sunday Compass*, October 30, 1949, Magazine, p. 14.

RODMAN, SELDEN. "Ben Shahn," *Portfolio* (The Annual of the Graphic Arts), 1951, pp. 6-21.

RODMAN, SELDEN. "Ben Shahn: Painter of America," *Perspectives USA*, Fall 1952, pp. 87-96.

LOUCHEIM, ALINE B. "Ben Shahn Illuminates," *New York Times*, August 30, 1953, Section 2, p. 8. ("Artist makes drawings for Off-Broadway production of three plays called 'The World of Sholom Aleichem.' ")

BARR, ALFRED H., JR. "Gli Stati Uniti alla Biennale: Shahn e de Kooning—Lachaise, Lassaw e Smith," *La Biennale di Venezia*, April-June 1954, pp. 62-67.

LIONNI, LEO. "Ben Shahn, His Graphic Work," *Graphis 62*, 1955, pp. 468-85. (Includes selection from *Paragraphs on Art;* cover of issue by Shahn.)

MOE, OLE HENRIK. "Ben Shahn," *Kunsten Idag* (Oslo), No. 1, 1956, pp. 30-52, 56-58. (Text in Norwegian and English.)

PECK, EDWARD S. "Ben Shahn, His 'Personal Statement' in Drawings and Prints," *Impression*, September 1957, pp. 6-13.

B., A. "Portrait: Ben Shahn," *Art in America*, Winter 1957-58, pp. 46-50. (Photographs of the artist at work by Fernandez.)

"Ben Shahn," in "After Hours" [a column], *Harper's* Magazine, December 1957, pp. 79-81. (Discusses Shahn's illustrations for *Harper's* articles.)

WERNER, ALFRED. "Ben Shahn," *Reconstructionist*, October 3, 1958, pp. 16, 19-22.

COATES, ROBERT. "Should Painters Have Ideas?," *The New Yorker*, March 14, 1959, pp. 154-55. (Review of exhibition at The Downtown Gallery.)

HALE, HERBERT D. "Ben Shahn," *Art News*, April 1959, p. 13. (Review of exhibition at The Downtown Gallery.)

KRAMER, HILTON. "Month in Review" [a column], *Arts*, April 1959, pp. 44-45. (Review of exhibition at The Downtown Gallery.)

WERNER, ALFRED. "Ben Shahn's Magic Line," *The Painter and Sculptor*, Spring 1959, pp. 1-4.

GOLDEN, CIPE PINELES. "Ben Shahn and the Artist as Illustrator," *Motif*, September 1959, pp. 94-95.

FARR, DENNIS. "Graphic Work of Ben Shahn at the Leicester Galleries," *Burlington Magazine*, December 1959, p. 470.

Review of exhibition at Downtown Gallery, *Art News*, November 1961, p. 20.

GILROY, HARRY. "A Happy Response to Ben Shahn in Amsterdam," *New York Times*, January 21, 1962, Section 2, p. 17. (A report of the exhibition circulated by the International Council of the Museum of Modern Art.)